D1126224

## Dedication

To my mother, Juanita, my wife, Layla, my sister Eva and my children Kevin, Karel, Traci, David and Neda.

# Introduction

Whoever you are, wherever you are, whatever your convictions, welcome to life as I have lived it and seen it. Life's Reflections: Poetry for the People can be best described as an eclectic collection of vernacular poetic narratives, full of insights and surprises. The compositions are mostly rhyme with some free verse. They cover a wide cross section of topics that allows you to see me, yourself, your family, or your friends in the probing subjects expressed. Each narrative is accompanied by a captivating painting or photograph that illustrates the message. I am indebted to a host of artistic supportive friends whose creative images so enhanced this book.

I know that poetry is not a bell-ringer on the cocktail party circuit. If you ask the regulars of that group where they rank poetry on the list of desired conversational topics, most would give you a sarcastic laugh and tell you that on a scale of 1 to 10 that poetry gets a minus 1. The expressed disdain is frighteningly salient: "It's too esoteric," "It died in some Greenwich Village coffee house in the 1960s," "It's really boring," "I can't get into it," "It's mental masturbation," "It has no role in everyday life," "I didn't like it in school and I have no use for it now." STOP! I've heard it all.

I promise you this presentation will not bore you, in fact, you will enjoy the indulgence into the fascinating world of rhyme, meter, metaphor, symbolism and free verse. It is my hope that Life Reflections: Poetry for the People will be a dynamic, entertaining and uplifting experience in your life. The wide spectrum of areas covered, include love, women, sports, psychiatry, travel, music, family, jazz, relationships, the 1960s and more.

I am eternally grateful to my English Literature professor at the University of Notre Dame, Father Chester A. Soleta. Decades ago, he shocked me into a reality I had never known. On the first day of class, he dynamically announced that it was his pleasure to guide us through the maze that is English Literature. Father emphasized that poetry was his specialty and he would make it "live in our souls." Making good on his promise, he introduced us to poet T. S. Elliott, by dramatically reading his composition, The Love Song of Jay Alfred Prufrock. That sharing is indelibly etched on my mind. The reading changed my world, engendering a lifelong love of poetic expression. Thanks, Padre

# Tommy Hawkins
# Biography

One of the Nation's leading eclectics, Tommy Hawkins has enjoyed an incredible career as a two-year Notre Dame basketball All-American, a ten-year veteran National Basketball Association player and player representative, a college lecturer, a pioneering Golden Mike and Emmy Award nominated radio and television broadcaster, a public relations executive, and Los Angeles Dodgers Vice President of Communication. A civic leader, Hawkins' West Coast community involvement includes serving on the Boards of Directors of the Center Theater Group, Los Angeles Sports Council, Los Angeles Friends of Recreation, Children's Burn Foundation, Friends of Jazz at UCLA and was named Ambassador to the Los Angeles Unified School District's Adopt a School Program.

His numerous awards include being inducted into the Chicago Sports, Illinois Basketball, and the Los Angeles Athletic Club Halls of Fame. He has also been honored as a 'Treasure of Los Angeles, Notre Dame Alumnus of the Year,' Franciscan Communicator of the Year and received the National Newspaper Publishers Association's Russwrum Award. Hawkins is one of Los Angeles' most requested speakers.

# Thoughts

Sometimes the beauty of life overwhelms me;
the joy of a song, the whisper of the wind,
the warmth of the sun, the smile on the face of a friend,
a hearty hello from a stranger, a loving hug tenderly
rendered by a baby, or the caress of the woman who
wants only to be with me.

When I experience these things, I shout to the
heavens "Thanks, God!"
You see, in this world of conflict, chaos and
one catastrophe after another;
in these hostile states of structured détente and other
forms of supposed coexistence and in light of
economic struggle, racial conflict and social
injustice, one's sanity must be kept.

Despite social and technical advances, man's
sustaining state of emotional well-being
lies not in the mad pursuit of money, power and
success, but in those things that money can't buy
and governments can't legislate.

©LeROY NEIMAN'S NBA ALL-STAR GAME

# Knights of the Roundball Realm

Four nights a week they take the court,
proud sons of delighted mothers.
The chosen who survived 'the cut,'
now most of them are 'brothers.'
Well trained and primed for battle,
they thrive on competition,
living out their boyhood dreams
avoiding the feared attrition.

With armor stuffed with lots of cash,
they trek from city to city,
Knights of the Roundball Realm
who perform for the rich and the pretty.
Hardwood gladiators holding court at modern arenas,
living life in the fast lane
with little time for novenas.

The constant screech of moonshoes
accent their darting moves,
amazingly they're airborn
in unstoppable zone-like grooves.
A ballet on the wild-side danced
at a hectic pace,
high-wire slammin' and jammin'
that's up close and in your face.

Descendants of historic stock,
great names of legend and lore:
Big George, Wilt, Elg, Russ,
The Cus, Big Blue, Big O and more;
Bald Eagle, Jerry, Hondo, Doctor,
Pearl, Clyde, Nate and Rick,
Kareem, Magic, Larry and Hawk
all made the Kingdom click.

So sound the mighty trumpets
and let the banners fly,
for the Knights of the Roundball Realm
are about to go gliding by.
Resplendent in royal colors
they'll give you thrills galore,
all hail their grand arrival
as they proudly take the floor.

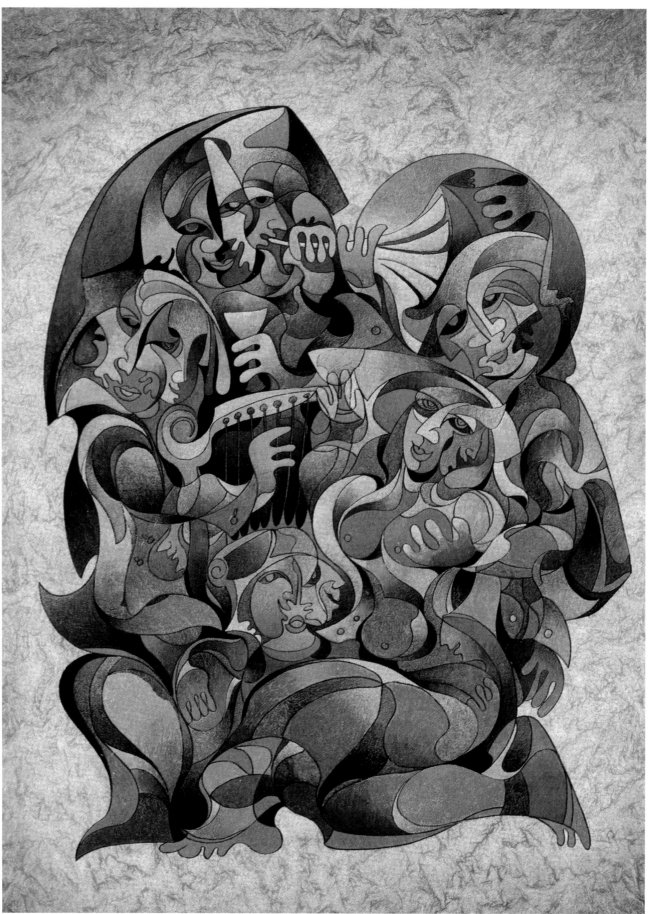

LOVE SONG

# Music of My Mind

Life's melodies invade me,
some archival as they flow,
encircling mind and body
with movements to and fro.

Orchestral operettas
dramatize the changing scene,
then come enticing nocturnes
so Angelic and serene.

Incessant scores of music
paint the images I'm seeing,
cascading compositions
that bathe my very being.

Polytonal phrases pour
from instruments galore;
percussions, keyboards, woodwinds, brass
and strings that touch my core.

Sonatas, fugues and canons
blend with Jazz and lots of Blues,
an amplified fantasia
with Big Bands I often muse.

A constant stream of sensate sounds,
modulations self contained,
no preludes or finales
just passages sustained.

God's gift to my humanity
so diverse and beatific,
I praise the Eternal Maestro
so giving and prolific.

FATHER OF PSYCHOANALYSIS SIGMUND FREUD

COURTESY OF ARTIST TIM TOWNSLEY

# Psychoanalysis

Flipping ruffled pages of reminiscent scenes,
waking up the echos of past nightmares and dreams.
Kaleidoscopic scoping of the windmills of your mind,
drifting in a universe not knowing what you'll find.

Happy times and heartbreaks dart swiftly through your head,
memories that you cherish and others that you dread.
Multi-colored footlights illuminate the stage,
with scenes that bring you pleasure, but then there's also rage.

Gigantic floating puzzle with a thousand moving pieces,
psychic galleria decked with flowers and with feces.
Rapid fire slide show, oh don't tell me you've forgotten,
how some things are so beautiful and others so damn rotten.

Searching every cranny for connections you must find,
some are quite apparent, but to others you are blind.
Disciple of Magellan, charting stormy, choppy seas,
mapping your existence while contemplating pleas.

Peeking through the keyhole at the things that shaped your past,
their impact on your future leaves you spent and so aghast.
Confusing yet revealing, a process straight from hell,
welcome to your twilight zone, Sigmund's show and tell.

# Yesterday's Gardenias

Yesterday's gardenias and freesias are all gone,
yet their aromatic presence so distinctly lingers on;
enticing sensory magic that flows wave after wave,
inviting our indulgence in the fantasies we crave.

Jasmine and plumeria that once beautified the place
with florid coloration adding dignity and grace,
are now just faded flowers that succumbed to daily strife.
Somehow there's no place for them in a crowded hectic life.

We no longer whiff sweet ginger or inhale a fragrant lei,
I miss the powerful pungency that we've come to hold at bay.
Bring back the effervescence that once circled my whole being
and release the floriculture that has mesmerizing meaning.

"Where have all the flowers gone?" I've heard so many sing,
voicing the need of adornment that pretty blossoms bring.
Gently caress a bouquet of beauty, partake in petals galore,
and when they die and lose their form, go out and get some more.

THE FIRST                                                    COURTESY OF ARTIST CRAIG PURSLEY

# Jackie, Do They Know?
## (An Ode to Jackie Robinson)

Do they know what you did Jackie Robinson when you broke that color line?
Do they know the worlds that you opened when the Dodgers asked you to sign?

Do they know the humiliation that you suffered through the years, or how it felt to
'stomach' the threats and constant racial jeers?

Do they know the competitive passion with which you played the game, or the
host of insults you endured when they defiled your name?

Do they know that you rose above it with majestic winning style, escorting a
perennial bridesmaid down the coveted championship aisle?

Do they know you were a 'Black Moses' with soul of raging fire, a man who firmly
stood his ground with undiminished desire?

Do they know that you had all the tools: talent, 'smarts,' and skill, well blended
with civility plus an unshakable iron-clad will?

Do they know that when you left the game no grass grew under your feet, you
continued pioneering using the executive suite?

Do they know with respect and reverence, we document your deeds, careful to
water and nourish your bountiful well-sown seeds?

Do they know that in the Hall of Fame you regally reside, having scaled the
heights of the "Grand Old Game" and humanity with pride?

Do they know that you left us early, age 53 when you passed?
But in that great half-century, what a legacy you amassed.

14/245     "Girlfriends"

# Masquerade

Lost in a masquerade
going through the paces,
living lies that can't come true
sporting phony faces.

Tripping under starlit skies
trying to make it real,
digging in for all you're worth,
but just can't get the feel.

Wanting to let it all hang out,
go for the gusto they say,
but knowing full well with each tick of the clock
things just aren't that way.

Laughing at jokes that don't amuse you,
feigning an evening's delight,
smiling until your face is tired
straining with all your might.

Match play in a loser's game
of social tinker toys,
will he be your Prince Charming?
or just another one of the boys….

Yes, lost in a masquerade
confused, but you keep on trying,
for being out among them
beats the hell out of sitting and crying….

JAZZ PAINTINGS

# I Dig Jazz

Perhaps you think me esoteric
or some "too hip" music cleric.
I'm not an avant-garde barbaric
but play me please those notes generic.

Now folks, before I'm mis-construed,
I'm not a far out bebop dude,
nor a narrow-minded prude,
jazz is my life-long interlude.

Jazz has the sounds of my soul's essence,
which I feel is the quintessence,
with a sparkling effervescence,
I demand its constant presence.

So cast away your consternation
and process this information.
It's a simple realization,
I need free form syncopation.

# Ground Zero

Screaming terror in full flight
hell bent on annihilation,
unmitigated hatred
seeking instant ruination.

Horrific death of thousands,
stench of evil every where,
headlines blast "Grave New World,"
we watch with frozen stare.

Heinous inhumanity
measured to the very minute,
insidious mass murder,
heed the message and find who sent it.

Barbaric act of treachery
diabolically surreal,
fanatic death of fire
fanned by phony religious zeal.

Echos of Adolph Hitler
reverberate Ground Zero,
as they dig for those who perished
hero after hero.

The world shakes its troubled head
in total disbelief,
while New York mourns lost loved ones
gripped by agony and grief.

'Vengeance is mine' sayeth the Lord,
states my bible as I read,
with every justification
please exercise God's speed.

CASINO

# Life's 'A Bitch'

It's not wrong to dream of fame,
your name in lights and fan acclaim,
but face it folks you know it's true,
seldom do we get our due.

So many times we've listened to
the just missed tales of the near to do,
with fortune right within their reach,
it washed away on a sandy beach.

But we revere the rich and famous,
like some slick and cunning "Amos,"
waiting for ships that never dock,
but when they do, we'll be out of hock.

It will happen just you wait,
that jackpot's going to set us straight;
so hold on to your lucky ducket
and pray to win the golden bucket.

Fat chance you say, that might be true,
but what are working folks to do?
We roll the dice and check the ticket
and tell the boss where he can stick it.

So onward sir, and you too lady, spin that fortune wheel,
for one day Monte Hall will ask "Are you ready to make a deal?"
Wake the town and tell the people, you're about to wear the crown,
for the announcer has just called your name and
asked you to "come on down!"

SKETCH BY ANDY COX

# Let Me Be Your Man

Let me be your sun.
The warmth that penetrates the pores of your skin
and sinks into your cosmic soul,
the rays that caress and tan your body,
the light of day that brings a smile to your face
chasing the clouds and enriching the earth.
Let me be your sun.

Let me be your wind.
Wind that whispers in your ears and blows your long
flowing hair,
wind that chills your body and makes you
want to cuddle,
the invisible power that spins your windmill
and brings a song to the trees,
nature's force that commands your attention.
Let me be your wind.

Let me be your rain.
Rain that falls upon your face and drenches your body,
rain that makes you want to frolic on the beach
or forces you inside for an indescribable afternoon
of love and ecstasy,
rain that brings you to a window to peer out
as it dances on the surroundings.
Let me be your rain.

Let me be your moon.
A full moon of radiance and majesty
lighting the way to a world of loving feelings,
a moon in which you can lose yourself and
fulfill all of your fantasies,
the celestial illumination that you can see
on an evening walk, or from your bedroom window
on a warm love-filled night.
A moon you can wish upon.
Let me be your moon.

Let me be to you all the things a man can be
to a woman without illusion or false grandeur.
Let me share with you all of the wonders of nature and the world
in a glorious relationship of love and harmony,
Let me be your man.

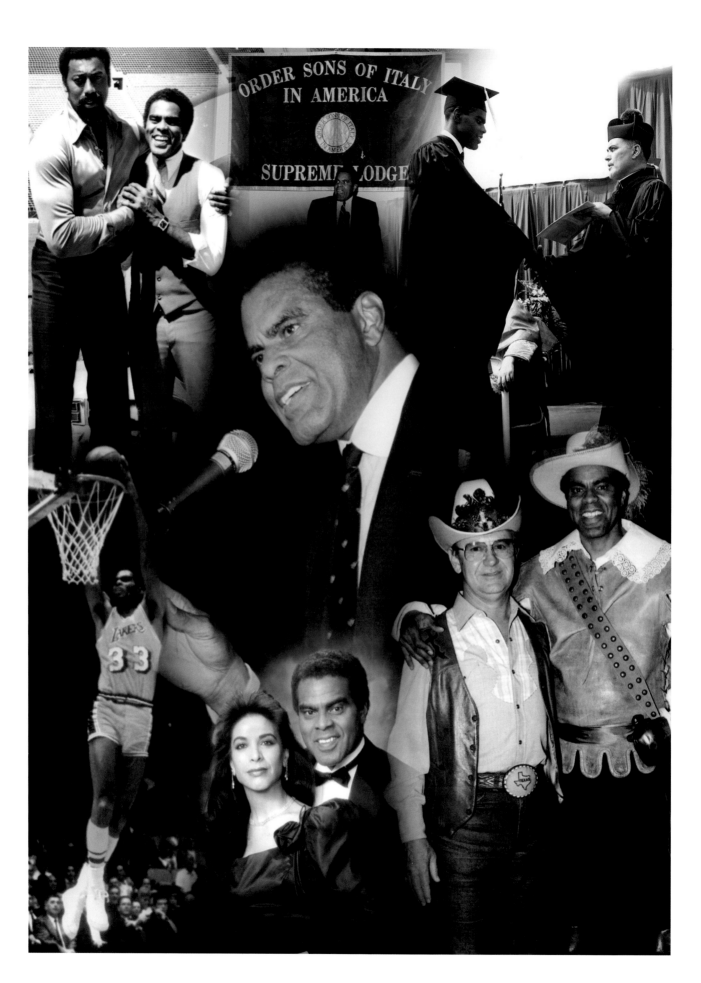

KABC RADIO
TOMMY
HAWKINS

# Recapitulation

Memories can often haunt me and refuse to go away,
in this world of recollection I find myself today.

Gazing at old photos, reliving days and nites,
probing magic moments, tugging at fallen kites.

I do my best to reconcile the eclectic life I've led,
reaching for puzzle pieces that are dancing in my head.

I know I can't go home again or keep the music playing,
yet recapitulation sometimes sends this hound a baying.

Foolishly, I revisit episodic interludes,
then deal with life's realities that so factually intrude.

What would have happened if?  My God, what a senseless game!
but I still insist on petting this beast I will never tame.

THE
AMAZING
AMANDA
AMBROSE
HER SONGS...HER PIANO

# The Search for "Manda Brose"
# (Amanda Ambrose)

Many folks have touched my life, I love them goodness knows,
they shared with me their humanity and left with me their prose.

They nurtured my existence; in my vase they placed a rose,
and strolled with me down many paths and other roads we chose.

I've lost contact with so many, they say that's how life goes,
but help me friends, I've got to know, what became of 'Manda Brose?'

With lusty voice she'd fill a room with rich engaging song,
capturing each demanding ear from the sound of the opening gong.

Seated at the piano, she embraced her melodies,
and with gifted style and flashing smiles, invoked our reveries.

Enberg would say, "she touched them all," her repertoire was vast,
from the new and futuristic to haunting things of the past.

She made us shout and holler then coaxed our salty tears,
we flocked to hear her magic and bathed her with our cheers.

Uniquely creative and 'twinkling with fun' she'd soar to heights above,
singing 'too ra loo ra loo ra,' then 'Please Send me Someone to Love.'

"Amazing Amanda" the critics claimed and applauding crowds agreed,
that this prolific songstress was a rare and precious breed.

Lady of soul with heart of gold; unforgettable? You bet.
It's been decades since I last saw her but, Amanda, you don't forget.

Please help an old nostalgic fool so this chapter I can close,
and tell me pray do, whatever became of the wonderful "Manda Brose?"

# Embers

Embers glistening in the night
with captivating glow,
inviting a fixation on the things
you've known and know.
Flickering remembrances stimulate
reflective juices,
forcing concentration on the
reasons and excuses.

Warm inviting embers that won't
let you turn away,
from the myriad of memories
cascading as you sway.
Suspended in a time machine
of virtual reality,
sailing on the open sea
with no time for banality.

The hearth becomes your private stage
where your heart and soul can dance,
and the mind delights in this
wondrous scene
and applauds you as you prance.

Like the sparks, you dart from here to there
engaged in the dying fire,
consumed by the introspection
that embers can inspire.

A soothing calm comes over you
replacing agitation,
having sipped the magic nectar
you praise the smooth libation.
You marvel at the mystic role
in which you've just been cast,
was it back to the future or
forward to the past?

CARNIVAL

# Carnival

There's something about a Carnival
that brings a town to life,
a light-infested 'turn on'
a drummer and a fife.

A wonderland for young folks
and a break for mom and dad,
a release from all the boredom
and the 'hum drum' life you've had.

A Ferris Wheel, the Carousel,
the Spinning Tilt 'O Whirl,
a chance to get much closer to that
very special girl.

Step right up, win a kewpie doll
or a cuddly well-stuffed bear,
perhaps a floppy Raggedy Ann
with colorful pigtailed hair.

It's a haven for the macho man
who wants to show his muscle,
and a playground for the low-life
to exercise his hustle.

Onion smothered sausages
and cotton candy galore,
plus a host of chanting game folks
inviting you to score.

We've been waiting, pretty lady,
and gentlemen, come on in;
don't miss this extravaganza,
the show is about to begin.

REVEREND THEODORE M. HESBURGH C.S.C.                    COMPLIMENTS OF THE UNIVERSITY OF NORTE DAME

# The House of Hesburgh

## A Salute to Father Theodore M. Hesburgh, President Emeritus, University of Notre Dame

Welcome to the House of Hesburgh – it has no walls and yet it is a fortress of humanity, intelligence and dignity.  It is a bastion of religiosity with windows open to the world. It is a place that you can go to restore your faith, talk and listen to your soul, chart your life's course and fortify yourself for the road ahead.

This home is filled with the love of God and our sacred Mother.  It is a storehouse of forthright conviction, understanding and sage advice, honed by years of education, fervent prayer and effective living.

It is well decorated with mementos of an eclectic past.  It features an endless array of both national and international awards and photographs documenting a life of historic accomplishments.  It is a place where the echoes of the past miraculously blend with the hope of the future.

This wonderful homestead is landscaped with the beautiful flowers of spring, the green leaves of summer, the radiant change of colors of the fall and tinged with the blustery winds and swirling snows of winter.  It is in every respect a place that stirs your being and inspires the spirit within you.

As you leave please go in peace, and upon departing, know that you have experienced the wonders of God through one of the most powerful and enlightened vicars of our time.  Rest assured you will never forget that you have visited the House of Hesburgh.

COURTESY OF THE SUGAR RAY ROBINSON FAMILY

# Sugar Man

In the violent pugilistic world
he was the 'Sugar Man.'
'Pound for pound the greatest'
swift of foot and fast of hand.
Dashing, sleek and mobile
folks loved his flashy style,
and the classic combinations
that he threw with cunning guile.

A middleweight from Motown
whose talents had no bound.
From welter to light heavy
they stood up, he set them down.
A masterful technician with incredible dancing feet,
and anyone who saw him, said Ray Robinson was "sweet."

A champion of the people who deserved the adoration,
with a flare for the dramatic, he delivered excitation.
But please don't think the Sugar Man was just a pretty face,
he dished out brutal punishment with such amazing grace.

A Captain Marvel of the ring whose cape was ever flowing,
and the aura that surrounded him was forever glowing.
A fighter of the century who fought such classic thrillers;
La Motta, Turpin, Bassillio, Olsen,
and of course some non-descriptive fillers.

Five times he wore the middleweight crown,
no opponent beat him twice.
Four times he regained the title
having paid the punishing price.
A fistic Hall of Famer who fought long
beyond his years,
Ray came to know fans' pity
but he also knew their cheers.

From ring ovation to youth foundation
he lived to please the crowd,
this legendary warrior did his best to make them proud.
He's a fighter for the ages, a darling of the fan,
pound for pound the greatest,
he was the Sugar Man.

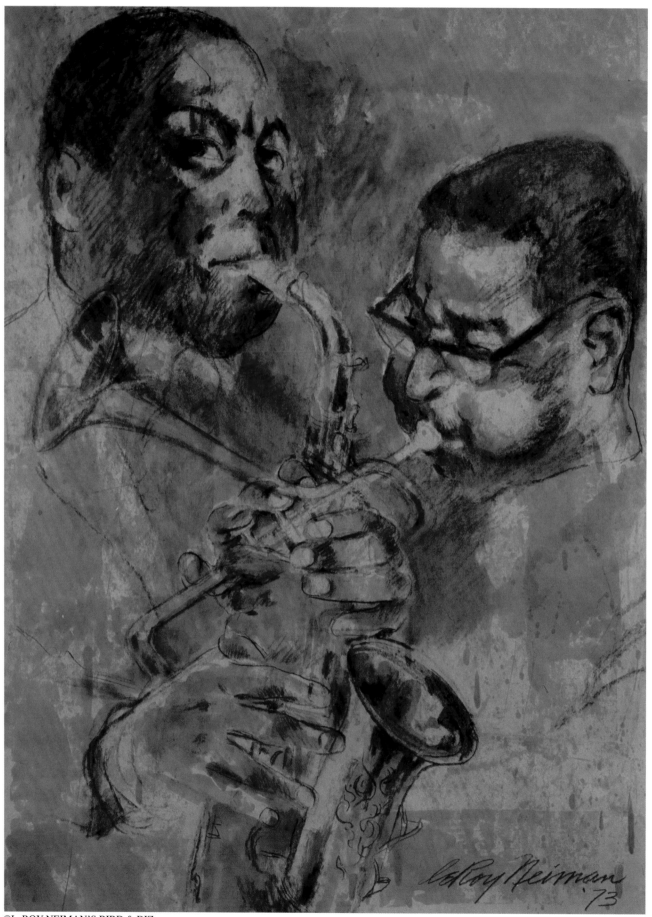

# We Free Kings

We Free Kings, the Magi of Jazz
led the reformation,
Bird, Monk and Diz entrenched
in change delivered emancipation.
Breaking restrictive shackles,
pied pipers of salvation,
we preached a brand new litany
all praise improvisation.

Exploring the depths of a brave new world
we broke away from swing,
propelled by expressive freedom
where the heart and soul's the thing.
Whether played on a chosen instrument
or 'music' that you sing,
we ignored the accusations
'it was just a free-form fling.'

Day and night we'd experiment
in search of a brand new bag,
and when the critics first heard it
they gave it a 'Be Bop' tag.
Folks strained to understand it,
we ignored the acceptance lag,
facing the staunch resistance
we played on, but refused to brag.

Soaring Birds of Paradise
in the skies of free expression,
inviting the flocks to follow
session after session.
Innovative, bold and creative
indelible winged impression,
new found province unrestrained,
no notes bared and no concession.

We free kings, now in Gabriel's band
look down on a world of fusion,
and smile at the nuveau avant-garde
and computerized collusion.
That change is inevitable
we face with no illusion,
and cheer the modern pioneers
and their world of sound profusion.

FAMILY PHOTO OF MY DAD

# The Burial of a Slightly Known Man

Aboard a giant bird I fly, the south my destination,
my trip sad but special, one that needs some explanation.
I'm off to pay my last respects to a man I've hardly known,
sick and disillusioned, John S. Hawkins died alone.

A man of great potential, pretty wife and children five,
a handsome man, intelligent, athletic and alive.
Yet somehow he became confused and lost his family passion,
and pretty wife and children five a new life had to fashion.

Five and twenty years have passed since that departing day,
and all the family members have existed in their way.
But death can sometimes bring to light forgotten untold things,
and in its harsh reality hidden truths it brings.

Arriving at the funeral home full of mixed emotion,
I viewed the body of this man, quite void of devotion;
I wondered why he chose a life that stripped him to the core,
robbing him of family, dignity and more.

But I did not come to judge him, my own life will have its turn,
yet perhaps in this sad story there's a lesson I can learn;
for when my day is up and dear ones gather in my den,
let them praise my contributions not moan what should have been.

The funeral was attended by the folks who knew him best,
who along with his five children laid him evermore to rest.
He is buried on a hillside in a grave next to his mothers,
with a tombstone placed above his head to distinguish him from others.

I left the grave with heavy heart, my eyes fixed on the ground,
I wondered what in life I missed with this man not around.
But hindsight is frustration, why dwell on what was not,
or stamp the earth in anger for the things I never got.

Aboard a giant plane once more, the west my destination,
a hundred thoughts race thru my head, I'm full of concentration.
In case you wonder why I fret or take the time to bother,
the deceased John S. Hawkins happened to have been my father....

FAMILY PHOTO OF MY MOM

# Thanks, Mom

How can we ever thank you for the life, the love, the zeal;
for the loyal dedication that has shaped the way we think and feel.

For your strength, your warmth, your wisdom that has led us through the maze;
our ever present beacon, penetrating every haze.

You have loved us so intensely, always caring, always there;
we adore you, special lady, and love to touch your hair.

Your smile has energized us and we've known your furrowed frown;
but through all our stress and struggles you have never let us down.

You filled us with such passion for the roads we've had to travel;
and never let us fall apart when we started to unravel.

Working to exhaustion ever mindful of our cause;
you gave us your last penny without ever taking pause.

Steadfastly you encouraged us, we always heard you say,
"you're as good as anybody; where there's a will, there's a way."

We marveled at your zest for life and love for all its people;
with open arms for everyone, like a church and stately steeple.

We praise you, Oh Great Captain, iron maiden with velvet touch;
and thank you so profusely, we love you oh so much.

So when there's talk of kings and queens or any reverent other,
we kindly ask that it includes our resplendent mother.

©LeROY NEIMAN'S SELF-PORTRAIT

# Neiman

Spanning the globe with a sketch pad
in search of inspiration,
lasered in on subjects
and the soul of artistic creation.

Mustached painting nomad
in a New York state of mind,
style in evolution
life's essence redefined.

Jazz man with a paintbrush
improvising on a theme,
sequestered in a Brownstone
stroking a visual dream.

The world comes alive on a canvas
in colorful profusion,
stunning abstract expressions
with impressionistic illusion.

Resident artist for Playboy,
drafting the Wide World of Sports;
Africa, France, Monte Carlo
and other exotic ports.

Dashing, Jet Set, bon vivant
with palette elevated,
spectrum in full motion
seldom understated.

# Bill McQuitter

Where have you gone, Bill McQuitter? My memories are all so clear,
it's been years since I last saw you, you remain a King in my sphere.

Black man of strength and integrity, and with the torch to light our fire,
urging us kids to grow up with pride, respect, conviction, verve and desire.

I remember when I first met you I was ten years old at the time,
you have no idea how I feared you when you started in to chime.

"McQuitter's my name" you bellowed "but I've never quit in my life,
and I'll paddle the butt of he who gives in to challenge, stress, strain or strife.

"I'm a teacher, a coach and advisor and I've got a job to do,
come heaven, hell, or high water I'm gonna make a man out of you.

"Now, some of you will 'fight' me, and others resort to tears,
but later on you'll thank me, when the months turn into years.

"I've got lofty expectations; some say I'm a mean 'black dude,'
but in behavior, dress and manners a positive image you will exude.

"The world is no place for a weakling, dig in and give it your all,
pick yourself up and get back in the race if you happen to stumble and fall.

"And listen 'jokers' don't cross me or put me in some 'trick bag,'
for I will guarantee you your ass I'm gonna tag.

"Now toe that line and lift your heads up and get your tails in gear,
so you can make some contributions when you get out of here."

It's been decades since those grade school days when McQuitter reigned supreme,
laying the foundation for young boys' hopeful dreams.

I've lived by those early lessons with a life-long goal to achieve,
employing the standards laid down long ago in which I firmly believe.

Wherever you are Bill McQuitter, I hope that you are proud,
because of your dedication, I've always stood out in a crowd.

FROM THE MOVIE SATURDAY NIGHT FEVER

# Racing with the Moon

Racing with the moon
Midnight Cowboy in despair,
decked out in his 'finery'
with tonic on his hair.
Shirt opened to the navel,
on his neck a chain of gold,
checking out 'the action'
if I may be so bold.

Lady killer on the loose
sucking down a beer,
looking for a woman who will
let him hold her near.
Lasered in on every glance
'Mr. Goodbar' on the prowl,
certainly there's a chick around
that will listen to him howl.

Smoothly he surveys the scene
with calculated motion,
smiling here and winking there
when he has the notion.
Fly-casting in the Disco using social bait,
will he get a nibble?
He can hardly wait.

The night turns into morning,
the club's about to close,
and his last chance at 'some action'
has just turned up her nose.

So, he downs his draft and starts to leave
reeling in rejection,
all alone and needy
with no hope of resurrection.
Hey, there will be another time,
a more seductive day
when he will leave the nightclub
having swept some 'skirt' away.
But, tonight he simply must accept

there will be no horn of plenty,
like the mug left sitting on the bar,
Don Juan had come up empty.

DESIRE

PHOTOS BY TOMMY HAWKINS

# New Orleans

Mississippi river 'Dahling,'
queen city of the South;
home of jazz and Mardi Gras
"honey, shut your mouth."

Music is your heartbeat,
rhythm is your time,
great food your constant promise,
over indulgence is your crime.

Great legend of the Bayou
with sultry steamy air,
a throbbing undercurrent
and a gourmet bill of fare.

Creole dreams and Cajun queens
will decorate your place,
while riverboats and banjos
accent the Southern grace.

Louie, Bix, and Alphonse were
nurtured in your cradle;
while Morton, King and Bolden
served jazz from your tasty ladle.

Pete, Al, and Winton
maintain that living lore,
while Branford, Sally and Randy
keep them coming back for more.

The French Quarter holds them spellbound
with its multitude of songs,
a captivating Lorelei
for the ever pressing throngs.

May your saints always go marching in,
as the ole' Miss flows to the sea;
and always save another
stroll on Bourbon Street for me.

THATS LIFE

# That's Life?

Card game with the daily faces
playing tens but faking aces,
dockets jammed, too many cases,
"dopers" trying to hide their traces.

Crying out with primal scream
because some "ass hole" ruined your dream,
black coffee ma'am, please hold the cream,
who cares if salmon swim up stream?

Battered women and child abuse,
insane people on the loose,
don't give me reasons, there's no excuse,
I see the engine but where's the caboose?

Years of hope and family pride
crushed by teenage suicide,
dinner served up with cyanide,
a moment of silence for those who died.

Feminist gains versus male frustration,
doused by pills and frequent libation,
angry men crying out castration,
should they consider masturbation?

Homosexuals in gay profusion
on parade in grand illusion,
fighting AIDS a deadly intrusion,
coping with the mass confusion.

Leaders lying through their teeth
double dealing from beneath,
faking remorse while laying the wreath,
piercing sword without a sheath.

Horny psychiatrist on the make,
control the mind then the body take,
prepare yourself for the next earthquake,
please, no candles on the cake.

# That's Life?
## (Cont)

Merger mania grips the scene,
old monopoly with a brand new sheen,
inside traders vent their spleen,
Wall street business from the latrine.

Tainted chicken, fish and ham
down our throats the merchants cram,
then there's the Iran-Contra scam,
does anybody give a damn?

Parked on freeways going nowhere,
eyes fixed in a gridlock stare,
no relief from the pressures there.
Whatever happened to Sonny and Cher?

Where's that hope for which we cry?
That Shangri La before we die.
Planes colliding in the sky
above the spray for the old med fly.

**SUSAN GOODMAN**
**MRS. AMERICA 1983**

# Mrs. America

You're lovely, Mrs. America,
jeweled queen with radiant smile;
wearing the crown in glory
with a husband to share your style.

Elegant lady in flowing gown
with tears streaming down your face,
the folks back home are ecstatic
to know you took first place.

The cameras flash, there's wild applause,
the crowd is shouting your name,
and people around the country
can share in your claim to fame.

Yes you're lovely Mrs. America,
heartbeat of all we cherish,
living a dream in grandeur
which I'm sure will never perish.

For a year you'll reign in splendor,
the toast of the marital set,
serving notice to the nation
Mrs. Goodman hasn't lost it yet.

# The Person in the Mirror

There you are, check it out,
visual image head to toe.
Face to face with reality
that's only partially so.

Reflection right before you
fills the mirrored space
up close and personal, one to one,
then comes the psychic chase.

Is what you see what you get?
Oh no! Cries a voice from within
Dealing with this dichotomy
is where the fun begins.

Is what's revealed truly real,
the essence of your being?
Or must you say to a care-less world
what you see is not all that you're seeing.

WINDY CITY

# Sleepless in Chicago

It's three o'clock in the morning and sleep isn't on the menu,
wide awake in Chicago as I contemplate my tenure.

A glistening moon on Lake Michigan lends an iridescent glow,
creating ripples in my mind of memories long ago.

All alone with my music in the still of a nippy night,
man without a mission who enjoys a reflective flight.

It was in this vibrant city that my die was cast,
I'd like it if you'd join me as I wander through my past.

First stop, Altgeld Gardens where our life was rearranged.
"The Gardens" was once a haven, but I'm told that all has changed.

At Carver Elementary School I grew up really fast,
the foundation of my present where I got the things that last.

My teachers were unforgettable: Seaberry, Robinson, Gant and McQuitter,
and my cherished grade school sweethearts who had me all a twitter.

A toast to all my buddies from the early hood:
Letch, Wally, Tenchie, and Stoops, we were bad, but we were good.

Thriving city on the move, integration at ol' Parker High:
Coaches Kramer, O'Farrell, and Toben always standing by.

Track star Jess Owens who came to speak at our school,
and his daughters Marlene and Beverley who made the fellas drool.

A DEEP DISH PIE IN...
CHI-TOWN

# Sleepless in Chicago
## (Cont.)


Seventy-first and South Park Ave, now Martin Luther King;
prep hoopsters came to hone their game high above the ring.

Park City with Organist Sterling Todd, roller skating the hours away,
charming the fine young ladies as we tried to make our play.

The DJs that we listened to Messers Daley, Kent and McCoy,
and the popular Al Benson with his verbal "hoy poloy."

There was jazz from every sector thanks to Lewis, Jamal, Hancock and Harris,
and clubs a plenty, citywide a virtual musical Paris.

Saturday jaunts to the marvelous "Loop" were my weekly passion,
trumpet lessons, record shops, and Baskins to shape my expanding fashion.

Trips to the Art Institute, the Aquarium and Brookfield Zoo,
Wrigley Field and Comiskey Park, seeing baseball's well-to-do.

Square dancing at the Band Shell, the Bud Billiken parade,
Polish sausages beneath the "El" where we could catch some shade.

Ice skating on the Midway, first date at the London House,
Fifty-first and Drexel Square where I courted my first spouse.

Leading the city in scoring, four year "ride" to Notre Dame,
sell-out crowds at the Stadium and All-American fame.

Yes, Sleepless in Chicago riding waves of days gone by,
God, I love this city, there're so many reasons why.

To Tommy
Best Wishes
June Lockhart

# June in December

Oh Lady of Christmas within our midst,
a luminous star high on our list,
reigning queen of the yuletide season
all wrapped in smiles, feeling and reason.

June in December with twinkling eyes
and a joyful soul that your face belies.
Belinda Cratchet you did play
and that fervent spirit never goes away.

We've watched you for years and we love how you function;
Lassie, Lost in Space, and Petticoat Junction,
The Yearling, Sergeant York, and The White Cliffs of Dover,
and the tens of other movies more over.

Lilting Lady dressed in Christmas gown,
why is it we've never seen you frown?
Within our manger we behold
a zest for life that's as pure as gold.

Angel on high, a candle glow,
Jingle Bells and soft fallen snow,
these are all notions you inspire
as we sit before our Christmas fire.

You will never be a dying ember,
not as long as we remember
those wonderful feelings you impart,
that come directly from your heart.

We celebrate and spread good cheer,
sing Auld Lang Sine and cry in our beer.
'Tis the season to be jolly, mistletoe and boughs of holly,
Deck the Halls, bring on the folly.
Weren't you the Lady with the Collie?

# The Traveler

Just saying that I like traveling
grossly misstates my style,
better to say I crave the road
and applaud each tenth of a mile.

I'm a modern day Marco Polo,
Magellan had nothing on me,
never lived a man with suitcase in hand
who hits the road with such glee.

Traveling is my way of life
and I've got stories untold,
I can hardly wait my next venture
and the escapades that unfold.

Now I'm not knocking home life,
for everyone needs a base,
but I belong to the moving-on breed
and I've got to state my case.

The world is a wondrous playground
with toys too numerous to mention,
and to get my hand on as many as I can,
my friend, is my life-long intention.

Now I know you've been a status quo Joe
but your life needs a major correction,
set some time aside and give it a ride
the map goes in every direction.

©LeROY NEIMAN'S BIG BAND

# Now You 'Has' Jazz

Black forefathers played the game, Kufumbana was its name,
free expression was the goal, unbridled renderings of mind and soul.

Brought to America, harnessed and chained, a remnant of dignity that remained,
sustaining force for the suffering slave who used his music to keep him brave.

Expressing every phase of life, including sorrow and the strife,
plaintive songs from young and old, the only safe way to be bold.

Storyville with its bayou beat, Dixieland jazz in sweltering heat,
Basin Street blues in basic black, Creole rhythms racked 'em back.

Darktown strutters in syncopation, pulsating beat served with libation,
tenderloin district in New Orleans, the place of history-making scenes.

Sharing in the early glory were Joplin, Oliver and Kid Ory;
but don't forget whatever you do, Armstrong, Handy, Bix and Picou.

Twentieth Century on the move, recorded jazz put in the groove.
Big Band fever grips the land, blacks and whites put on the stand.

"Play as written" was the theme, dimming free musicians' gleam.
Structured music was devised, restricting those who improvised.

Unfulfilled, they played and dreamed, for a freer way they schemed,
jamming feverishly non-stop, till Bird and Diz came up with bop.

Jimmy, Art, Benny and Fats, Count, the Duke and all the cats,
Monk, Trane, Dave and Miles played the jazz that brought the smiles.

Yes, at first misunderstood, "crazed musicians up to no good."
Sounds improvised right to the core, freedom at last, forevermore.

Bold expression unrestrained, every mood therein contained.
Get down, get mad, be happy, create, embellish, get hellish, pontificate.

Living from the soul within, talent once linked up with sin,
a slice of life for all mankind: Musical Mecca of the mind.

Kennedy elected by narrow margin

Beatles invade America

Negro sit-ins integrate lunch counters

Mao launches Cultural Revolution in China

Jazz scene loses Coltrane

First flight of Concorde

Multitude hears King: I have a dream

250,000 Viet Nam war protesters march in capital

Mankind makes its greatest leap: To the moon

John F. Kennedy shot dead in Dallas

Berlin cut in two by Communist wall

10,000 hippies rally at New York Be-In

Glenn is first American to orbit earth

Race riots rage in Watts for five days

Police battle mobs as Democrats meet

Celtics win 5th straight NBA title

Thousands overwhelm Woodstock festival

Maris exceed the Babe's total by one

Koufax sets record with four no-hitters

American Negroes star at the Rome Olympics

Chubby Checker has us all doing the twist

Bobby Kennedy is killed

Freedom Riders beaten

Black power advocates call for revolution

Martin Luther King killed

LBJ signs Civil Rights Act

# Sixties (60s) Revisited

People of the sixties, please let me make this clear,
it's time to re-evaluate those years that you hold dear.
A recapitulation with no intent to smear,
although at times you'll feel the heat, I don't intend to sear.

Decade of the mushroom and dawning of Aquarius,
better life through chemistry and other things nefarious.
Come on, turn on, drop out, they cried,
no need to be vicarious, get with the psychedelic age and let the spirit carry us.

Were there reservations when you took that plunging dive?
I guess you bought that endless rap of flower power jive.
Were you just a nameless drone within a massive hive?
And at the time, I'll bet you thought the sixties would survive.

The home of the brave and the birth of the free,
a new set of rules with a better decree,
help Mother Nature plant a tree,
"You were blind, my friend, but now you can see."

Hendrix filled your probing minds with scintillating sound,
Dylan was your troubadour with messages abound.
Joplin belted earth songs for the masses on the ground,
while Coltrane played his favorites for the avant-garde around.

Lofty evocation, wild gesticulation, verbal masturbation,
non-stop demonstration, outright confrontation,
social constipation, sad assassination,
chemical sensation, commune habitation,
free-love fornication, Richter-like vibration,
challenging the nation.

"Would be" prophets scoured the land,
magic moments in their hand,
leading Sergeant Pepper's Band
urging all to take a stand.

Acid heads in altered states demanding to be heard,
shouting protestations, some of truth and some absurd.
Counter culture in full flight, both VIP and nerd,
soaring through the heavens like some predatory bird.

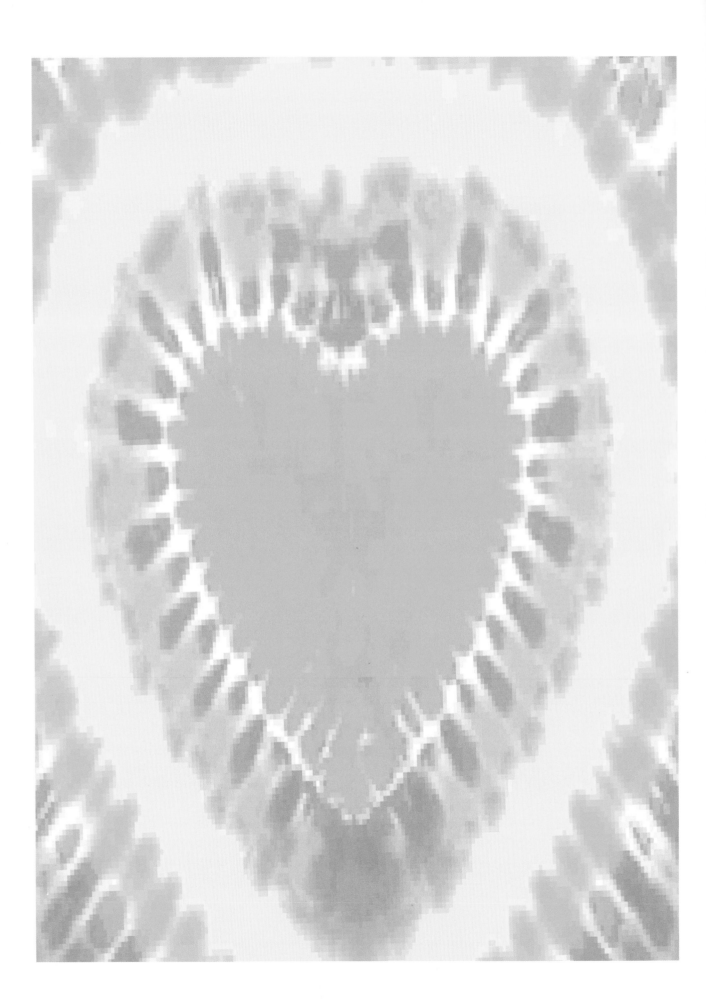

Floating minds on drug-fueled trips,
LSD on quivering lips,
faded jeans that hugged your hips,
curving roads with frequent dips.

Those speed launched jaunts to outer space
had no controls to set the pace,
and as you soared they called you "Ace,"
but you saw things you couldn't face.

Peaceniks, hippies, beatniks, yuppies marching in parades,
saviors of the universe with no time for charades.
Zealots of the higher cause just like the old Crusades
in colorful profusion came the Leary-led brigades.

Tell me, where did things go wrong?
Who bent the fork and snapped the prong?
Who softened up the protest song
and stroked the deafening ending gong?

And on the era, as we dwell
from love and peace to Manson's hell,
how do you rate it, please do tell,
as in your minds the memories swell.

The Hoffmans and the Ginsbergs and the Rubins were quite clever,
and the shock waves of 'The Sixties' will reverberate forever.
Could it ever be again?  Most folk will tell you never,
and from those gripping ties that bind,
I'm sure you'll never sever.

The crushing throngs at Woodstock have secured your lasting fame,
The Haight in San Francisco, mates, will never be the same.
The Windy City shivers from the mention of your name,
and history reminds us that it wasn't just a game.

So there you have it in a stack,
The Oracle, the Digger, and the phony guru quack.
Is there a bridge from speed to crack,
and do you want the Sixties back?

# Neda's Rubber Ducky

Little rubber Ducky floating
freely in my tub,
I wonder what you're thinking
as you watch me sit and scrub.
Just cruising through the bubbles,
not a worry, not a care,
you know I'd really miss you
if ever you weren't there.

You seem so happy, Ducky,
in this water wonderland,
and whenever I reach out for you
you're always right at hand.
My Dad says you were with him
when he was just a tot,
and you never made a single sound
when the water got too hot.

How I wish I had your life style
just drifting to and fro,
you're never in a hurry
but always on the go.
Bobbing at your leisure
you take away all tension,
and I tell you all my secrets
which I'm sure you'll never mention.

You're the captain of my water way,
protector of my port,
and even when I splash you
you're always such a sport.
Let me tell you something, Ducky,
no matter what my path,
there'll always be a place for you
when I take a bath.

# Does She Exist?

Does she exist, this lady
who will steal my heart away,
taking me forever
from these frantic games I play.

Will she touch my cosmic soul
and end my rambling days,
zapping my defenses
with penetrating rays?

Will she be short and cunning
with a smile that I will prize,
or will she be tall and leggy
with a face I'll idolize?

Will she be young and perky
The essence of shining youth,
or will she be older and wiser
with beauty, wisdom and truth?

Will I be her Prince Charming
that she searched for day after day,
or just a personal respite
that she took along the way?

Will I be hit by a thunderbolt
and succumb to her stunning force,
or will she simply say hello
and proceed as a matter of course?

Is this all Sir Lancelot's dream,
some hope of Camelot
a self-imposed indulgence
an unnecessary plot?

Does she exist is the question
that for now I'm going to table,
for I've got to get back to my dating
and dispense with this incomplete fable.

LOVERS

# Could It Be?

Dancing ribbons in the skies,
soft warm sunsets in my eyes,
moonlight glowing up above,
could it be that I'm in love?

Time goes by but I don't know it,
inner strain, try not to show it.
Counting doves but never sheep,
yes, it's difficult to sleep.

Reveries my favorite scene
from it happiness I glean,
but loneliness is hard to bear
when the lady isn't there.

Utopian thoughts twirl in my head,
nights without her I just dread,
but gorgeous flowers line my way,
along another cloud nine day.

Candle light and sparkling wine
to her lovely eyes adds shine,
elegant and so serene
living this romantic scene.

Surrender to her warm embrace,
kisses gently bathe my face,
turn out the lights, fold back the spread,
we are wonderful in bed.

In living passion bodies sway,
there is no time, there is no day,
aloft in never ending space
dead heat in a lover's race.

Is this the one to God I pray?
Please don't let her go away,
a gentle push, a caring shove,
could it be that I'm in love?

# Ode to the Sons of Troy

It was a game to be reckoned on October twenty-second
under a bright Indiana sky.
Sixty thousand had gathered at old South Bend
and there was a good reason why.

The sons of Troy, well trained to destroy
Decked out in their colors grand,
On high they came to old Notre Dame
equipped with a marching band.

The mission at hand had been carefully planned
by nightfall the story would be told,
how again USC, with uncontrolled glee,
had embarrassed the blue and the gold.

Awaiting the gong some ten thousand strong
Trojan rooters from far and near,
arrived on the scene in support of their team
lending voices in lusty cheer.

The campus was jammed and at home people crammed
to watch the great clash on TV.
The spectacle loomed as the bass drums boomed,
a classic of royal decree.

The forty-ninth renewal of the cross-country duel
was about to get under way,
the odds had been stated and the Trojans top rated,
but that would be changed on this day.

For the past ten years with shamrocks and tears
the Irish bemoaned their fate,
as hard as they tried success was denied
losing seven of ten to this date.

Coaches Robinson and Devine with the same thing in mind
fought the tension that gripped their chest.
Each man in his way with his own dues to pay,
professed that his team was the best.

The folks in the stands yelled and clapped their hands
and drank spirits to keep them roaring.
They were all well prepared for the glory to be shared
and they knew it wouldn't be boring.

# Ode to the Sons of Troy
## (Cont)

For search if you will the valleys and hills,
but you won't find in any direction,
competition as keen or a more dynamic scene
than the Irish-Trojan connection.

Two highly ranked teams with championship dreams
ran on to the gridiron green.
From the crowd came a roar for the game just in store,
the players were taut and mean.

What a game!  What a day!  What excitement!  What play!
One worthy of Knute and the Gipper:
running here, passing there, in the flat on a flare,
well charted oh Devine Irish Skipper.

There was Ken MacAfee who in every degree
is an All-American strong,
bulling his way, he came to play
and caught passes all afternoon long.

And oh Susanna that Joe Montana
was magnificent calling the shots;
in total command he passed and he ran
hitting Trojan vulnerable spots.

Messers Browner and Fry playing sky high
were in constant pursuit of Rob Hertel.
They had both made amends to seal off the ends
and their tackles made Trojan blood curdle.

Wearing bright Kelly green, the mean Irish machine,
sons of Notre Dame all;
on defense led gladly by Burgmeier and Bradley
had an absolute Trojan ball.

Amid thunderous cheers and the toasting of beers
Notre Dame fans shouted the score.
Forty-nine to Nineteen, magnificent scene,
Katy, bar the door.

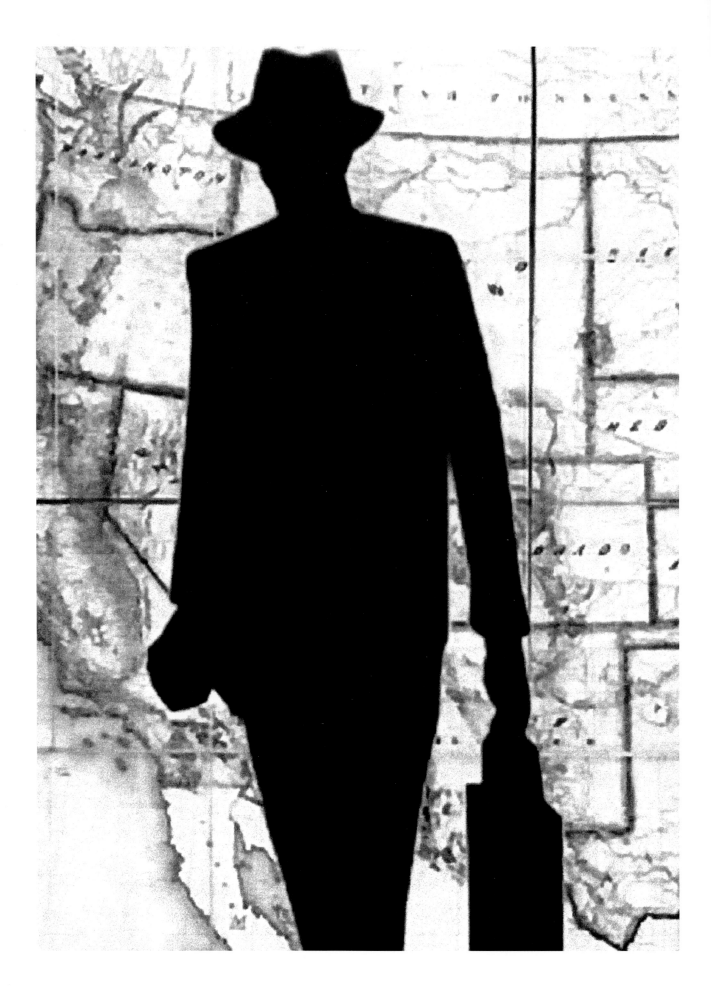

# Traveling Man

A traveling man will often say
the road is lonesome, stay away.
But ask him when he feels no pain,
what a change in his refrain.
Of New York he'll marvel
its people, its sights,
the splendor of Broadway
its millions of lights.
The clubs in the village
and quaint little shops,
the social whirl that seldom stops.

A traveling man will often say
the road is dreary, stay away.
But while relaxed at a late bull-session
what a change in his expression.
The splendor of Hawaii, he will extol
a balmy breeze, a Waikiki stroll,
the wonder of Pele and Diamond Head,
girls in grass skirts, the food he was fed.

A traveling man will often say
the road is depressing, stay away.
But when lifting a cool one at his favorite tap,
tales of his travels he must recap.
San Francisco is one of his favorite cities,
restaurants, Chinatown, oriental pretties.
North Beach is exciting, he likes cable cars
and Fisherman's Wharf under the stars.

A traveling man will often say
The road is weary, stay away.
But as much as it pains him to leave his abode,
it's damned exciting to be on the road.
For there he finds just where he belongs
despite the wine, women and songs.
He learns to relate and where things are hollow
and the hook, line and sinkers he shouldn't swallow.

If you're tied up in knots and you want to unravel
give yourself a chance to travel.

ANNIVERSARY

COURTESY OF ERNIE BARNES FAMILY TRUST

# Life's Reflections

Free will is our constant companion, in life's game of players' choice;
a chorus of billions with lusty refrains in which we all have a voice.

When your world unfolds before you, will you view it with never a cringe?
Will the angels on high adore you or be shocked by your life-long binge.

When all of the traveling is over and your fast-lane life is through,
you will sit in retrospection of the things you've done and do.

Will your past reflections grip you and rip your soul apart?
Leaving a hollow feeling, as you long for a brand new start.

Or will a smile fill the lines on your face as you recount each mile after mile;
recapping the pleasures of bygone days and a life of substance and style.

The maestro has played, you've danced to his tune and the piper must be paid.
His fee, my dear friend, depends in the end, on the types of moves you have made.

From swing to waltz you've not missed a beat, Gliding across life's floor;
Has it been an empty, long song and dance with some steps you'd rather ignore?

Predestined by rights of passage, from birth to day of rest,
we battle life's ocean to stay on course, as our sun disappears in the west.

So, before darkness engulfs you, and the winds of death call your name,
give some serious thought to your life style, to ignore it would sure be a shame.

DESTINATION UNKNOWN                                    COURTESY OF ERNIE BARNES FAMILY TRUST

# Hope

In this time of pleading screams
where worldly woes unroll in reams
and problems overflow their streams
somewhere there's a field of dreams.

In this state of pressing need
with motivation fueled by greed,
where barren lands have gone to seed
is there a gentler, kinder breed?

In this world of 'in your face'
it's push and shove in the great rat race
to find that private special place
clutching cans of protective mace.

In this era ruled by dispassion
where being crude is quite in fashion
and it's not chic to show compassion
the homeless wait to get their ration.

In this day where ego thrives
we forge ahead despite the cries
searching for honey in queenless hives
entertained in dim lit dives.

For those not chosen for the teams
left out of life's successful themes
on whom the love light seldom beams
some where there's a field of dreams.

# Acknowledgments

Make no mistake about it; we get by with lots of help from our friends.  I'd like to thank the team of great people that made this book possible: Sue Townsley who lent technical skill and patience in shaping the manuscript, Richard Fischer at FireFly Digital Graphics, and Ed Profumo at Colorgraphics, Los Angeles, CA. for their professional guidance and tenacity in organizing the layout, Carlos Vargas at Collective Color for leading me through the endless print solutions, and Laurent Lainez for designing and painting the captivating cover of my book.

Hats off to the highly creative artists whose paintings so vividly visualize the messages: the internationally acclaimed LeRoy Neiman, Tim Townsley, Ernie Barnes and his representative Luz Rodriguez, Anatole Krasnyansky, Andy Cox, Michael Hall, Linnea Pergola, Aldo Luongo, Craig Pursley and Charles Fazzino.

Special thanks go out to John Heisler, Sports Information Director at the University of Notre Dame, all my friends at Art One Gallery in Santa Monica, CA. (Helen, Michelle, Sheir Randall, Frank Ponder),  Melissa Ranieri and Fernando Linhares, David and Elaine Marmel of the Mrs. America Pagent, the William McQuitter family, Zavier College publicity staff, photographer David Jedda, the wonderful and supportive executives and staff at the Museum of Tolerance in Los Angeles, Ca. (Rabbis Marvin Hier and Abraham Cooper, Liebe Geft, Beverly LeMay, Lorranice Sair and Avra Shapiro).

It pays to advertise and no one does it better than public relations specialist Bob Mazza